ABRAHAM LINCOLN

BY
AMY
L. COHN

AND
SUZY
SCHMIDT

PICTURES BY
DAVID A. JOHNSON

SCHOLASTIC PRESS
NEW YORK

SEE THAT TALL, TALL MAN

in that tall black hat? Know who he is? That's right, he's the man on the penny — Abraham Lincoln, sixteenth president of the United States.

Was he always that way, straight as an arrow, tall as a tree, serious as can be?

Let's go back. Let's go back a ways, and see.

Look. In the cradle. See the baby? That's Abraham Lincoln, born on a cornhusk mattress one cold Kentucky morning. Big sister Sarah stands beside her new brother, waiting for him to grow.

And grow he did! From the first, Abraham was big. "Longshanks," they called him, and all his life his knees and nose got a little too friendly every time he sat down.

He's a boy of seven now. My, he's strong. Strong enough to plow and plant 'longside his pappy. Strong enough to swing an ax. Strong enough to help when the family moved to the new state of Indiana.

That first winter the Lincolns huddled in a half-faced camp. Just three walls and a roaring fire between them, the panther, the wolf, and the bear.

Those days, you could touch a tree with every step even if you walked a week. Abe knew that. He swung and swung his ax. The blade bit through white oak and sycamore. The felled timber became a cabin and a barn, the cleared land pastures and fields. Lots of those trees, lots and lots of them, made split-rail fences — horse high, bull strong, pig tight.

Years later Abe looked like those rails — worn and rugged, long and lean and lined. But not yet. No, not yet.

School? Wasn't much time for that. Abe did go —
by littles, he said, a day here, a week there, maybe a
year all told. He learned to figure, to read, and to
write. "That's my name," he showed cousin Dennis
with a grin. "Doesn't look a bit like me, does it?"

Abe listened eagerly when mother Nancy shared
the Bible's treasures or his daddy told a favorite yarn.
He could recite a preacher's sermon word for word
— act it out, too. He lay awake nights, worrying unfa-
miliar ideas until he got them right, and for good.
Enjoyed 'rithmetic so, he covered the cabin walls a
time or two with his reckonings.

And the sad, sad time after his mother died eased
when his new stepmother urged him to satisfy his
appetite for reading everything and anything, when-
ever he could.

Abraham read about Aesop's animals and Aladdin's lamp and Robinson Crusoe's shipwreck. He read about George Washington, our first president. He read while the plow horse rested. He read while he ate his lunch. Late at night, he leaned toward the dying light of the fire with a book in his hand. "My friend's the one who has a book I ain't read yet," he said, and he'd walk miles for the chance to borrow something new.

Abe was eighteen 'fore the chance came to see someplace new. He and a pal floated a flatboat filled with pork, flour, meal, bacon, and potatoes down the Ohio, down the Mississippi, down to New Orleans. For the first time Abraham saw men, women, and children sold like cattle from one owner to another. That was the way with slaves.

What could he do? Not a thing. Not then, anyway.

Abe was twenty-one, a man grown, when his father moved the family to Illinois. Abe saw his parents settled, said his good-byes, and set off across the prairie to the new town of New Salem, hard by the Sangamon River. There, folks with big plans for the future offered a place for a young man to make his way in the world.

What did he do in New Salem? What didn't he do! He ran a shop, but Mr. A. Lincoln told funny stories a whole lot better than he sold seeds and saleratus, and soon that shop "winked out."

Abraham studied surveying and served as a soldier. He roamed the roads delivering mail. He even minded babies. For fun, he joined the debating society and learned to convince others to come 'round to his way of thinking.

"Work, work, work, that's the main thing," he once told an acquaintance, and he worked as hard with his head as ever he had with his hands.

People liked the strapping, striving young Lincoln. Oh, Abe's pants were short, his hands big as shovels. Can't think anyone would have called him handsome. But when he ran for state legislature, those who knew him gave him their votes.

He lost, but that didn't much matter. Abe had struck upon the life for him. He'd be a legislator and a lawyer, too. He won the next three elections to the state assembly. Time to make the Illinois capital home for good.

In Springfield Lincoln practiced law in a roomy office overlooking the center of town. Every morning, he'd hoist his big boots atop his desk and read the newspaper — out loud. Sometimes, he'd pluck a paper from the mess, tuck it inside his hat, and race to the courthouse. Carry a satchel? Why bother? Abe kept his papers safe and dry up top.

Abe met and married Mary Todd, smart and sassy. Lincoln towered over his tiny bride. "We're the long and the short of it," the proud groom quipped. The couple bought a handsome house on Jackson Street, where they would treasure not one, not two, not three, but four baby boys.

Half the year Lincoln worked the county court-houses — riding the circuit, they called it. Didn't bother him spending nights two or three to a bed, nor having but a minute to confer with a client. And, in the evenings, when judge and juror, lawyer and defendant would crowd 'round the tavern fire, Abe kept 'em laughing 'til their bellies ached.

"That puts me in mind of the time I was walking along a dusty road and a farmer in his wagon passed by," Lincoln began. "'Would you be good enough to take my overcoat to town for me?' I asked. The farmer agreed. 'But how will you get it back?' 'No trouble at all,' I said. 'I'm going to stay right inside!'"

Mr. Lincoln also relished the travel between times. Gave him room to think.

Now look at Abraham, all dressed up and on his way to the White House. Abe had tried — and failed — to win a United States Senate seat. But, by golly, the speeches he gave about slavery and the country's future made him so famous that he found himself elected president just two years later.

It was time to bid farewell to his friends, and to Springfield. "To this place, and the kindness of these people, I owe everything," he told the crowd gathered at the depot. He asked for God's assistance, and their prayers. Then, he boarded a train headed east.

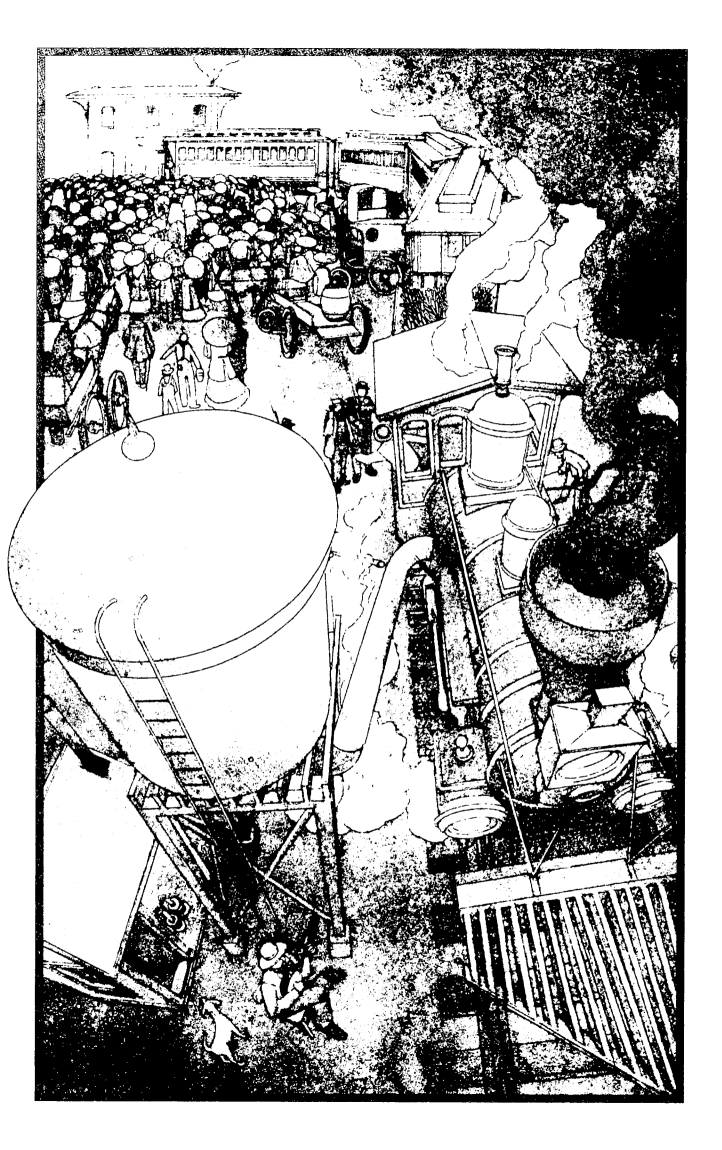

A powerful hard task lay ahead. The United States weren't united anymore. Some in the southern states disagreed so strongly with how much say-so the federal government should have, they formed their own country. They were concerned particularly with the right to keep slaves.

"A house divided against itself cannot stand," Lincoln believed. No government could endure half slave and half free. It will be one thing or the other, he said. Only war would decide, and Lincoln knew it.

Leading a nation at war was the hardest task of all his life. People died, too many to count. President Lincoln grieved each one. "Sometimes I think I'm the tiredest man on earth," Mr. Lincoln said. And he probably was. He slept in snatches, walking the streets at night, stopping by the telegraph office at all hours for the latest news. He comforted wounded soldiers from both sides and visited every Sunday with citizens desperate for information about loved ones.

Sometimes he turned up at meetings wearing slippers; his feet ached so. He often began by reading to his advisers from joke books. "With the fearful strain that is upon me night and day, if I did not laugh I should die," he told them.

His boys made him laugh, too. He tussled with them on the White House floors and let them keep goats on the south lawn. Once, he wrote an official presidential pardon for their pet turkey. Wouldn't do for Tom to become Thanksgiving dinner!

After nearly two years of war, Abraham Lincoln signed the Emancipation Proclamation, declaring all slaves free. "If my name ever goes into history, it will be for this act," he said, "and my whole soul is in it." *Abraham Lincoln,* he wrote slowly and carefully, for his hand was swollen and sore from greeting hundreds of New Year's Day callers.

Later, some urged the president to take back the proclamation. Lincoln refused. "I am a slow walker," he said, "but I never walk backward."

The bloody battles wore on. Lincoln seethed. In his youth, he had wrassled enough to know you had to fight a foe and finish him off, too. Finally, Lincoln chose General Ulysses S. Grant to lead the Union troops. Unconditional Surrender, they called Grant, and Grant would fight to win.

A year later the war was over. The union was preserved. Let us bind up the nation's wounds, Lincoln said, and he meant it.

Mr. Lincoln could only begin the healing. Five short days after the Confederate surrender an angry southerner shot the president as the Lincolns watched a play.

They took Abraham across the street and laid him on a cornhusk mattress. In a few hours, he was dead.

A train slowly carried Mr. Lincoln home to Springfield. The train stopped fifteen times. Each time, thousands gathered to mourn the last great casualty of the war.

More people stood along the tracks, silent and solemn, as the barefoot, backwoods boy — now grown, now gone — went past.

Look. There's Mr. Lincoln. There, in the building made for him. He sits quietly, eyes steady, knees high. Imagine. All his life he was so busy he barely had time to take a haircut. Now he rests.

He looks like a giant, doesn't he?

He was.

IMPORTANT DATES FROM ABRAHAM LINCOLN'S LIFE

FEBRUARY 12, 1809 – Lincoln is born near Hodgenville, Kentucky.

1816 – Lincoln moves with his family to Indiana.

1818 – Lincoln's mother dies.

1819 – Lincoln's father remarries.

1830 – The Lincoln family moves to Illinois.

1831 – Lincoln moves to New Salem, Illinois.

1834 – Lincoln elected to the Illinois State Legislature.

1837 – Lincoln moves to Springfield, Illinois.

1842 – Lincoln marries Mary Todd.

1858 – Lincoln runs unsuccessfully for the United States Senate.

1860 – Lincoln elected president of the United States for the first time.

1861 – The Civil War begins.

1863 – Lincoln signs the Emancipation Proclamation.

1864 – Lincoln re-elected president of the United States.

APRIL 9, 1865 – Peace signed at Appomattox Court House, Virginia, effectively ending the Civil War.

APRIL 14, 1865 – Lincoln shot by an assassin.

APRIL 15, 1865 – Lincoln dies. He is fifty-six years old.

FOR SETH, ABSOLUTELY — A. L. C.

FOR GRANDPA STUCKEY, WHO CELEBRATED THE SOUNDS OF WORDS — S. S.

TO BARBARA McCLINTOCK — D. A. J.

The authors gratefully acknowledge Beatrice Schenk de Regniers, who got us started, and George Cohn, who showed us the way. Special thanks to Jon Austin from the Illinois State Historical Society for meticulously fact checking text and art.

LIBRARY OF CONGRESS CATALOGING-IN-PUBLICATION DATA

Cohn, Amy L. • Abraham Lincoln / by Amy L. Cohn and Suzy Schmidt ; Illustrated by David A. Johnson.—1st ed. • p. cm.

Summary: A simple biography of the Illinois lawyer who served the country as president through the difficulties of the Civil War.

ISBN: 0-590-93566-6 • 1. Lincoln, Abraham, 1809-1865—Juvenile literature. 2. Presidents—United States—Biography— Juvenile literature. [1. Lincoln, Abraham, 1809-1865. 2. Presidents.] • 1. I. Schmidt, Suzy. I. Johnson, David A., ill. III. Title. E457.905. C62 2000 • 973.7'092—dc21 • 96-048709

10 9 8 7 6 5 4 3 2   02 03 04 05 06   Printed in Mexico 49   First edition, February 2002

David A. Johnson's art was rendered in ink and watercolor washes. The text type was set in 15-point ITC Century Book Condensed. The display type was hand lettered by David Coulson. Book design by David Saylor.